ISBN 978-1-330-07764-1
PIBN 10020111

This book is a reproduction of an important historical work. Forgotten Books uses
state-of-the-art technology to digitally reconstruct the work, preserving the original format
whilst repairing imperfections present in the aged copy. In rare cases, an imperfection in
the original, such as a blemish or missing page, may be replicated in our edition. We do,
however, repair the vast majority of imperfections successfully; any imperfections that
remain are intentionally left to preserve the state of such historical works.

1 MONTH OF
FREE
READING

at

www.ForgottenBooks.com

By purchasing this book you are eligible for one month membership to ForgottenBooks.com, giving you unlimited access to our entire collection of over 1,000,000 titles via our web site and mobile apps.

To claim your free month visit:
www.forgottenbooks.com/free20111

English
Français
Deutsche
Italiano
Español
Português

www.forgottenbooks.com

Mythology Photography **Fiction**
Fishing Christianity **Art** Cooking
Essays Buddhism Freemasonry
Medicine **Biology** Music **Ancient
Egypt** Evolution Carpentry Physics
Dance Geology **Mathematics** Fitness
Shakespeare **Folklore** Yoga Marketing
Confidence Immortality Biographies
Poetry **Psychology** Witchcraft
Electronics Chemistry History **Law**
Accounting **Philosophy** Anthropology
Alchemy Drama Quantum Mechanics
Atheism Sexual Health **Ancient History**
Entrepreneurship Languages Sport
Paleontology Needlework Islam
Metaphysics Investment Archaeology
Parenting Statistics Criminology
Motivational

ELIZA SPROAT TURNER

From the portrait by Cecilia Beaux

OUT-OF-DOOR RHYMES

BY

ELIZA SPROAT TURNER

PHILADELPHIA
PRINTED BY J. B. LIPPINCOTT COMPANY
1903

ELIZA SPROAT TURNER
From the portrait by Cecilia Beaux

OUT-OF-DOOR RHYMES

BY

ELIZA SPROAT TURNER

PHILADELPHIA
PRINTED BY J. B. LIPPINCOTT COMPANY
1903

COPYRIGHT, 1903
BY
THE TRUST OF THE NEW CENTURY GUILD

CONTENTS

CONTENTS

IN MEMORY OF
ELIZA SPROAT TURNER

"IT was only a rosy girl who now stepped from behind the hermit,—a simple child whose arm no strong angel would ever borrow to further his world-work, whose lips no courier from heaven would ever think to touch with his message of prophecy; a mere bud of a woman with the baby dimples not yet out of her round, soft arms. Yet, as she stood there in the halo of her innocent beauty, my soul fell down before her in ready, unreasoning reverence. I seemed to be floating on the golden waves of her voice, swayed with the grace of her every motion, caught in the sun-brown wonder of her hair.

"I saw but the flow of curls, and curves, and dimples, and the brown, liquid glory of young, soft eyes, and the living crimson delicately threading through the ripe, dainty flesh,—the whole inexplicable magnetism of perfect physical life."

These lines, written by Eliza L. Sproat and published in 1852, will now be read by many for the first time. Instinctively we turn from the fair young girl that she sketched so long ago in " Father Ronan's Angel" to the loving tributes paid by friends of her own youth who still survive her, wherein we see her " fair and frail, with softly gleaming eyes and hair like the tendrils of the vine," in her girlhood such a vision of delight that all the boys who met her were hopelessly in love with her.

Between the period of her imaginative writings, however, and the numerous duties and important work for humankind that she accomplished before her death, an angel had borrowed her arm to further his difficult work, and the weapon wherewith he strengthened it was Experience.

Eliza L. Sproat was born in Philadelphia in 1826. Her father, originally a Vermont farmer, came to Philadelphia and engaged in some form of literary work. Her mother was Maria Lutwyche, one of three sisters who came to Philadelphia with their parents from Birmingham, England, about 1818.

After her father's death, the young girl lived with her mother and brother. She taught in the public schools for several years, and in Girard College from 1850 until 1852. The poet Daniel Kane O'Donnell was one of her pupils there, and he often spoke of her with appreciation in his later days. She held high rank as a teacher and always retained a deep interest in the cause of public education. When " Quaint Corners in Philadelphia" was published, in 1883, Mrs. Turner contributed to it the chapter dealing with the public schools.

Her marriage to Nathaniel Randolph—an orthodox Friend of ample means who married " out of meeting"—took place in 1855. After a few years of happy married life, Mr. Randolph died, leaving her with a son, Archer, who was her only child.

For some years after this she shared her home with her mother, " a little, lovely, red-checked lady of high English birth and quality and gracious manners," and two intimate friends, Mrs. Margaret Burleigh and Miss Mary Grew. They composed a happy family, and the atmosphere of the home was wholly in sympathy with advanced thought on the subject of women being treated in their work and lives with the same respect and remuneration that is accorded to men; and for awhile Mrs. Randolph laid aside the pen and turned her attention to her young son and domestic duties and pleasures. The tender friendship that existed between her and Mrs. Burleigh is revealed in " An Angel's Visit."

Archer Randolph became a physician in Philadelphia, and was rising into eminence in his profession through original research when his sudden death occurred in 1887. He is survived by his wife, a son, and two daughters.

In 1864 Mrs. Randolph was married to Joseph C. Turner, a lawyer of Maryland birth. They had both gone to the relief of the Federal and Confederate wounded soldiers at Gettysburg to offer tender ministrations at that dreadful time, and the comradeship then formed lasted for nearly forty years.

They purchased at Chadd's Ford a handsome estate with historic associations. On the summit of a hill which overlooks a battlefield of Revolutionary days and the beautiful valley of the Brandywine was erected a stately mansion, which, as their country home, became famous for the true hospitality exercised therein. It was tendered to all, rich and poor, but the ones who needed help, irrespective of race, class, or condition, were the ones who made the strongest appeal to the infinite bounty of the mistress of the home.

The house in the county, Windtryst, was the chosen *home,* but the winters were spent in Philadelphia.

Mr. Turner died in October, 1902. For two weeks afterwards Mrs. Turner seemed like herself, frail as always, but triumphing over the weaknesses of the flesh by the indomitable strength of her will. In November came an unmistakable summons, which, although not responded to immediately, caused her to set her house in order and direct others to continue the work that she had planned with such care. She had waited to see her beloved Guild approach its twenty-first birthday, an age of discretion, before she gave it her last blessing and benediction.

She died at Windtryst on the 20th day of June, 1903. On the following Tuesday a sorrowful group of friends assembled there for the last time. The Rev. Frederick A. Hinckley read her own " Evening Thoughts" as the first part of a service impressive in its simplicity. She was buried at Longwood, in the cemetery belonging to the meeting-house which was one of the storm-centres during the days that preceded the Civil War.

No one could have judged by the serene expression of Mrs. Turner's face that she had surmounted trials which the bravest women would shrink from passing through. Those who knew her best say " she was a brave woman."

There was always a beautiful serenity about her,— the impression of " a heart at leisure from itself,"— always a quiet, steadfast working out of the finest and most desired fruit of culture—she always gave the best she had to the best she could; and what she gave—and the best of what she gave was ever her- self—always returned to her to be given out again with added possibilities.

Mrs. Turner was endowed with unusual literary ability, and wrote prose and poetry for a number of magazines and papers before her marriage in 1855. In the files of *Sartain's Magazine,* which was pub- lished from 1849 until 1852, may be found a num- ber of the poems which are now republished.

Mr. Turner collected a number of the published poems, and the volume of " Out-of-Door Rhymes' ' appeared in 1872. This is Mrs. Turner's only book. One reviewer said that no one could get from it the impression that she had borrowed anything from another mind or had ever read a book, so entirely original was the product.

Between 1850 and 1855 she contributed a number of prose articles to *The National Era,* of Washington (in which " Uncle Tom's Cabin" appeared as a serial in 1852), and other papers and magazines. One of

her first successes was " The Rooster-Pecked Wife,"
a delightfully witty prose sketch. For this she re-
ceived great applause, and it was widely copied at
the time.

In the files of *The Woman's Journal*, of Boston,
Massachusetts, may be found nearly all of Mrs. Tur-
ner's prose writings. No attempt has been made to
collect them. In 1887 appeared her longest story,
running through sixteen numbers of *The Woman's
Journal*. It is entitled " Nobody to Blame," and
sets forth almost tragically the difficulties that a
daintily-reared city maiden encounters when she be-
comes a farmer's wife and tries to work as his mother
worked; her isolation in not having " gentlemen"
to talk to; in the farmhousely discussions " to be
utterly ignored,—so utterly companionless,—to have
a mind that is never consulted, a will that is never
respected." And Nora, the heroine of this story,
tears up a poem that she has written, with the reflec-
tion, " No whining, however sweet, only words of
cheer and healthful inspiration, have a right to live
in verse."

She tossed her contributions lightly in every direc-
tion, apparently keeping no record of where they fell,
giving them out in the same bountiful way that she

always gave herself to the causes in which she was interested. There is a wealth of clever sketches buried away in the files of newspapers and magazines. One of her neighbors at Windtryst said that she used to watch eagerly for the *Delaware County American* in order to read Mrs. Turner's contributions to it. But Mrs. Turner seems not to have preserved them; and she procured with difficulty a copy of her collected poems when asked by one of the Guild members to present it to the library.

"Evening Thoughts" was published in *Sartain's Magazine* in 1849, but was much longer in the original form; and "Granny and I," a poem, appeared in *Graham's Magazine* in 1853.

She never did better work, from a literary standpoint, than that published between 1849 and 1853, with the exception of "An Angel's Visit." The little poem, "If," which she termed "From the Yankee," is a pure poetic outburst, unequalled perhaps by any other in her collected poems. It was published in *Sartain's Magazine* in June, 1852.

Her original way of stating old problems and new needs in writing annual reports was probably unexcelled by any secretary in Philadelphia whose duty it is to prepare these instructive documents. The tree, with all its branches rudely clipped off at top and sides for lack of space, with the pitiful wish, " If only I had room to grow," in one of the annual reports of the Guild, is a little masterpiece in the way of a visual argument in her plea for larger quarters for the Guild.

The summer before her death, Mr. Elder, a lifelong friend, paid a visit to Mrs. Turner at Chadd's Ford. She read to him a new story for children which she had written, that had not been published, and she also read to him a bird song, both of which were delightful.

A terrible accident had befallen her in 1868. Thrown from a carriage, she fell under the horse, whose heavy body lay across her own until she was rescued by some workingmen. Knowing that any struggle of the fallen animal would be fatal to herself, she had the presence of mind to seize the rein with one hand and hold his head firmly to the ground. She told Mr. Ames of the thoughts that passed through her mind: " This will not kill me; but I shall be permanently crippled and disabled—perhaps I shall spend years on a bed. Then I shall have the leisure I have long wished for, to mature my own thoughts, and to do or to dictate some real writing!"

The desire to write, to create in literature, never left her. Near the end of her life, in speaking of the little monthly paper published as the organ of the New Century Guild, she said as she outlined its possibilities, "I should like it to be a representative organ for women's interests and always hoped to work and write to this end myself; but I think you will understand me when I say that I have had a number of irons in the fire; I have been occupied with a variety of small things and never seemed to have the leisure that is necessary to write."

When face to face with Death all that one has accomplished looks small to the individual in that terrible search-light, I suppose; but Mrs. Turner could, more hopefully than many of us, leave the reckoning of her "small things" to God.

Life and its problems, especially the problems that women are called upon to solve in the living, appealed with great force to Mrs. Turner; and to adjust to some extent the balance that, to the optimist, it seems possible to strike between those who have and those who have not, was her life-work. Her sense of humor was too keen, perhaps, for her to be too radical a reformer, but her convictions were absolute and always stated with authority, whether she was on a winning or a losing side; and her wit enabled her to point the many and excellent contributions that she made to the cause of Equal Suffrage. These were so delightfully humorous and done so artfully that even the victims of her satire enjoyed them. Mrs. Turner identified herself with the Woman's Suffrage Movement in 1870, when the Pennsylvania Society was formed, by serving it as Corresponding Secretary. While she held this office only one year, she never lost her interest in the cause, and from time to time contributed poems and articles to newspapers and magazines on this subject.

In her youthful days she attended the meetings of The Philadelphia Union of Associationists, of which Mr. John Sartain was a prominent member. In 1847 they studied the works of Charles Fourier; and the value of systematic methods for the amelioration of social conditions was to Mrs. Turner a mainspring of action throughout her life. She always kept herself informed of helpful work undertaken in other cities, and if similar agencies were not in force in Philadelphia, she promptly set to work to organize them. Her power of organization was unrivalled. Her keen and critical observation of men and women helped her in the selection of competent persons to carry on the work that she had begun; and then she turned to the other duties that stood like sentinels ever as her shadows.

When she heard of the organization of a Country Week Association in a neighboring city, the idea appealed to her with great force. What was easier than to take tired women and children, deprived of all advantages, from superheated city conditions and give them a glimpse of her beloved country hills and woods and meadows? She investigated needs in the city and resources in the country. At first, the money expended and the hospitality extended were her own gifts—hers and neighbors' at Chadd's Ford and friends' in Philadelphia.

The personal attention given to this work in the early days by Mrs. Turner was a marvel to those who knew her. She seemed so frail that her duties as wife and mother and housekeeper would have seemed more than enough to tax her.

Looking up the needy children in the city, going with them personally to her home, and returning them, when the visit was over, laden with fruit and flowers for the mother, or the other children left behind, was at first her constant care.

The work grew rapidly, until it is now one of the

most important charities of the city. Of the good done, of the impetus given to live a different life, of the merit acquired by those who give, no estimate can be formed.

After the work of the Country Week Association had been fully launched, the Centennial was celebrated in Philadelphia. On the second day of the Woman's Congress, held during the Centennial, Mrs. Turner read a thoughtful paper, entitled "Women's Clubs," setting forth her ideas of what such clubs should be. "They should be primarily an association for personal convenience; that is to say, I should not start them for the furtherance of any 'ism, however interesting, nor yet of any charity, however laudable."

The prominent women who worked together in the interests of the Centennial had found this association so delightful that the suggestion to form a club along broad lines was received with enthusiasm. A meeting was called at the house of Mrs. J. Peter Lesley, "The Lady from Philadelphia" in the delightful "Peterkin Papers," and in 1876 the New Century Club was formed. Mrs. Turner was the first Corresponding Secretary and the third President. During the second year of the club's existence she went to Europe. All the impetus she gained from the trip went into the additional work she accomplished for others after she returned.

During the twenty-six years that intervened between the formation of the New Century Club and her death Mrs. Turner's connection with the Executive Board was uninterrupted, and her watchful care extended over its movements to the end.

One of her first inspirations during the new club's life was to form evening classes for those who were busy through the day. At that time there were few opportunities in the way of good evening classes and free libraries, and in a very short time Mrs. Turner perceived that if a club was a necessity for women who commanded their own time, so much the more must the needs of working women be expressed through club life; and the formation of the New Century Guild followed in 1882. This club, including at first chiefly young girls, has been more and more attracting thoughtful working women to its comfortable club life as Mrs. Turner's plans for it have developed.

In the interests of the Guild she found what became her life-work. To it she gave the best she had to offer,—her time, the benefit of her experience, and of her means, all with a bountiful hand. She was never happier than when solving problems for her girls and working and planning for them. When Mrs. Turner was seen at a Guild Board meeting, apparently intently gazing at a certain spot in the carpet, and seeming not to be cognizant of what was going on, those who knew her well knew that she was revolving in her mind some plan for the Guild that she would presently bring forth, but of the reception of which by the other Board members she felt somewhat doubtful. Miss Beaux, in her charming portrait of Mrs. Turner, which the members of the Guild commissioned her to paint, has caught this expression most happily. The portrait was painted in 1897 and was formally presented to the Guild in June of that year, when a memorable reception was given. The Portrait Committee was a self-appointed one, growing out of the strong desire of the Guild members to possess a worthy memorial of the devotion they bore to their Guild mother.

The Committee worked earnestly over the project, and in selecting one of the foremost portrait-painters of the day, and one who co-operated with them in their work of love, they secured a real work of art that is now the dearest possession of the Guild.

Advanced as ever in her thought, Mrs. Turner perceived that women working alone cannot obtain the greatest impulse in daily living. "I want men to join the Guild also," she said on one of those last days when she was putting her work in order before leaving it finally in other hands. She felt deeply that the best work is done and the greatest inspiration gained when men and women meet together naturally and rationally.

Of a friend of Mrs. Turner's, who has also just left us, and who was endowed like her with a gifted individuality, one who loved her best wrote soon after her death:

"She will continue to be the great, helpful soul that she was and is. Give her your loving thoughts as to one who still lives for those who love her: they will return to you with the added possibilities of her now untrammelled spirit. I do not at all think of her as lost to me; what she has been she will be— and more. How much more depends upon how much I am fitted to receive."

This is the summing up of influence. The members of the Guild have had the benefit of all the wisdom and the tenderest thoughts of Mrs. Turner. Upon them rests the responsibility to fit themselves to receive her message and to carry on the work she would have each one do. Each one her best, only her best!

From her earliest years she was passionately fond of Nature, and the love of all things beautiful was hers until the latest days of her life, when she watched for the last time the advance of summer from her favorite window at Windtryst, which commanded a beautiful view. She delighted in the cornucopia of wild flowers that Nature holds out impartially to all the children of men who seek her treasures, and a great jar of May-apple blossoms, with the leaves cut off close to the stems so that the beauty of the shy waxen flowers should not be hidden, appealed to her more deeply than the rarest orchids.

When she was a girl she was fond of roving over the mountains alone with Nature. In those early days her natural disposition was to be alone with books and her own thoughts.

As she sat dreaming in her maiden fancies, a fairy change came over her fortunes and put within her hand the golden key to enable her to scatter roses where there had been thorns. But the angel who guarded her must have trembled at times for her as he transfigured the dreamer into the Guild

In Memory of Eliza Sproat Turner

Mother happy in the love of four hundred daughters. To understand their needs, she must have had like desires; to give them comfort, she must have needed help; to inspire them with the desire to attain a life of helpful worth, she must herself have conquered the thorny by-paths that lead to The Heights.

Lenore M. Lybrand.

Philadelphia, 1903.

OUT-OF-DOOR RHYMES

❦ ❦

HOW THEIR CREEDS DIFFERED

BEDDED in stone a toad lived well,
　　Cold and content as toad could be.
As safe from harm as monk in cell,
　　Almost as safe from good was he.

And " What is life ? " he said, and dozed;
　　Then, waking, " Life is rest," quoth he;
" Each creature GOD in stone hath closed,
　　That each may have tranquillity.

" And GOD himself lies coiled in stone,
　　Nor wakes nor moves to any call;
Each lives unto himself alone,
　　And cold and night envelope all."

He said, and slept. With curious ear
　　Close to the stone, a serpent lay;
" 'Tis false," he hissed with crafty sneer,
　　" For well I know GOD wakes alway.

How their Creeds Differed

" And what is life but wakefulness,
  To glide through snares, alert and wise—
With plans too deep for neighbors' guess,
  And haunts too close for neighbors' eyes?

" For all the earth is thronged with foes,
  And dark with fraud, and set with toils:
Each lies in wait, on each to close,
  And God is bribed with share of spoils."

High in the boughs a small bird sang,
  And marvelled such a creed could be.
" How strange and false!" his comment rang;
  " For well I know that life is glee:

" For all the plain is flushed with bloom,
  And all the wood with music rings,
And in the air is scarcely room
  To wave our myriad flashing wings;

" And God, amid His angels high,
  Spreads over all in brooding joy;
On great wings borne, entranced they lie;
  And all is bliss without alloy."

How their Creeds Differed

" Ah, careless birdling, say'st thou so?"
    Thus mused a man, the trees among
" Thy creed is wrong; for well I know
    That life must not be spent in song.

" For what is life but toll of brain,
    And toil of hand, and strife of will—
To dig and forge, with loss and pain,
    The truth from lies, the good from ill—

" And ever out of self to rise
    Toward love and law and constancy?
But with sweet love comes sacrifice,
    And with great law comes penalty.

" And God, who asks a constant soul,
    He tries his creatures sore and long:
Steep is the way, and far the goal,
    And time is small to waste in song."

He sighed. From heaven an angel yearned:
    With equal love his glances fell
Upon the man with soul upturned,
    Upon the toad within its cell.

How their Creeds Differed

And, strange! upon that wondrous face
    Shone pure all natures, well allied:
There subtlety was turned to grace;
    And slow content was glorified;

And labor, love, and constancy
    Put off their dross and mortal guise,
And with the look that is to be
    They looked from those immortal eyes.

To the faint man the angel strong
    Reached down from heaven and shared his
        pain;
The one in tears, the one in song,
    The cross was borne betwixt them twain.

He sang the careless glee that lies
    In woodbird's heart without alloy;
He sang the joy of sacrifice:
    And still he sang, "*All* life is joy."

But how, while yet he clasped the pain,
    Thrilled through with bliss the angel smiled,
I know not, with my human brain,
    Nor how the two he reconciled.

OLD AND NEW

I KNOW a narrow forest path, that climbs
The mountain side, arched thick with chestnut
    leaves
And maple, and the black-green massive oak,
Guarding from highest noon their underworld
Of beauteous life that cannot bear the light—
A curious underworld of mild decay;
Each prone trunk, lying ever where he fell,
Enamelled with fine lichens, couched in ferns,
While, stitch by stitch, soft, broidering mosses make
His gay green shroud, pricked out with coral cups;
And each unseemly rotten gap is filled
With orange fungus, and the straight club moss
Spreads like a small pine forest round his feet.
Here, wandering all alone, I heard a voice
Where human voice was not; and, turning soft,
I saw a wonder: from a palsied oak,
Clothed half in leaves and half in thready moss,
Came an old Dryad, parting painfully
The stiff, time-crusted trunk that scarce could yield:
A woody, wheezing Dryad, with gray hair
Like that long threaded moss, and fumbling foot

Unused to motion; slow she climbed the hill,
I following; many times she paused for rest.
So, blinking in the unaccustomed light,
And gasping in the too live mountain air,
She reached at last an old forgotten lake,
Sunk in the mountain top—black, deep, and still;
Hard to approach across the quaking marge
Of treacherous seeming land that was not land
For all its green, but fair and dreadful bog,
Which, year by year encroaching, pushed the line
Of water-lilies inward, till the time
When they should close above that bald Undine
Who, wakened by the plaintive wheezing call
Of her upon the shore, emerged to greet
Her ancient crony, gazed uncertainly
Upon her, then, remembering wistfully
Her broken dream, would fain return; but, held
By something in the voice, stood doubtful still,
Pushing away a clinging leech, which straight
Returning, she desisted with a sigh.
   "And am I, then, forgotten by my friend?"
Said Dryad; "yet 'tis scarce a century
Since last we met; I cannot sure have changed?"
Slowly the Naiad, in a dreaming voice
That seemed far off:

" Not we; the world has changed.
This beauteous lake, once haunted by a god,
The burden of whose glorious songs we still
Might faintly hear—if any cared to hear,
Among the modern echoes; these fair shores
Whose very earth is precious with the print
Of stately footsteps, and whose every stone
Is written close with stories of the past—
All are forgotten; all the world is changed
Since you, the loveliest Dryad of the wood,
And I, the noblest Naiad of the wave,
Were recognized and worshipped,—all is changed.
What prestige have these raw-barked modern trees,
Plebeian, doomed to early menial use?
What birthright have these nameless mountain
    streams,
Galloping vulgar hoydens—night and day
They violate my silence; night and day
This clattering noise of brooklets hurrying down
To join the larger clamor of the streams—
The reckless, leaping streams, gone mad with haste,
That would not stand an hour to rest the world.
Their hateful voices call into my dreams;
Their worthless words forever agitate
My deep self-contemplation."

As she spoke,
A strange wild song rose clear through her com-
plaint:
Onward, merrily onward!
Nothing can check my way;
The crowding ferns bend over,
Wooing me back to play;
The threatening rocks rise tall,
On every side a wall,
Breaking my waves to spray;
But for me, I shall not stay.
See, I break from my thrall—
Foaming out from the darkness,
Into the crimson sunset
Merrily down I come.
Deep, deep in my waves
His face the hot sun laves.
All the hill is alight;
Every tree is a torch;
And all the air is flame.
Hark! that song of a stream
That rings through my daily dream;
It is the voice of my lover
Calling afar to me.
Onward, steadily onward!

Into the growing twilight,
Into the midnight darkness,
Out to the morrow's sunrise;
Ever with firmer feet,
Until we two shall meet,
And, this lone wandering over,
Our true life is begun
When the two lives clash in one.
Ha! I long for the shock;
I plunge from rock to rock,
And the plunges cost me dear:
But for me, elate
With the joy of my coming fate,
I suffer, and have no fear.
Hist, cease!
. . . A sudden dream of peace
Holds me in its spell.
Is it I, so deep and still?
Picturing on my bosom
Reed and bending blossom,
And my ever-following ferns?
Close crowd the alder bushes;
And the long rude bramble pushes
To the front; above me reach
The flat boughs of the beech,

Flecking my breast with shadows,
A thousand crimped leaf-shadows
Under the noonday sun;
And, out from beneath a stone,
Flashes a sudden silver,
And circles, and is gone.
And over, skimming low,
The jewelled dragon-fly
Vanishes and returns
And stands so motionless,
His life you scarce would guess;
And all is glad and still:
And through and through I thrill
With a thought I cannot tell.
Ha, I know! I see
My life that is to be.
It is truth; in that swift moment
The pulse of the far Ocean
Rose and sank in me.
Movement and silence.
Now a change awaits me,
Change, and noise, and pain;
Roaring and confusion—
Throes of dissolution—
Ah, the brink is near!

Old and New

I suffer, but have no fear.
Over—I swoon—
I darken—I die!
Down . . . Is it I
That lie so brokenly?
All my dark substance
Tortured into whiteness,
Shattered into rainbows,
Glorified with pain?
And can I rise again?
See, I gather my force;
Greatening on my course
Till, the first meeting over
Between me and my lover,
In blending we discover
Our mission toward the sea.
Is it to wander free
Ever through forest ferns?
Is it to dive unswerving
Into the dreadful earth,
Feeling our way in darkness
Toward a second birth
In some far unknown land?
Is it to sweep superb
Around some glorious city?

Or, stayed by wheel and curb,
Drawn into thousand sluices
For daily grudging uses,
In every house to stand?
Yet are we one, and whole;
The myriad-parted soul
Shall labor in joy and patience
For every human need;
Waiting its final meed—
Pure amid loathsome soiling,
Free amid slavish toiling.
Hark! I wake from my dream
To the sound of a nearing stream.
I know the call of my lover
Thundering down the gorge.
"You hear!" she said, with mild intolerant sigh,
But spoke to air; for Dryad, long ago,
Fearing the evening damp, had faltered home;
Unconscious that the mould had seized her hair,
And that a leathery fungus stout had sprung
Between her fingers, thinking she was dead.
Relieved, the Naiad turned, and sighing, sought
The lake-depth, where she hides from all things new,
And dreams of all things old. Above her, wheel
Near-sighted bats, that think the trees ill-placed

Because they strike against them: and, around,
The melancholy whippoorwills complain,
Wailing a wrong they never tried to mend.
Still deepens that marsh luxury of green,
Crowding the lilies inward, till the stems
Tangle her feet; and, " Am I lake or land?"
Sometimes she asks in sudden deadly fear:
And soon, forgetting, peers to shape the shore,
But cannot for the mists herself has raised;
Or strives to understand some rising voice,
But cannot for the echoes that repeat,
And add, and modify, and reproduce,
Until the voice is lost. Or, baffled so,
She feels about those slimy lily stems,
And fails to grasp, and lapses into dream;
While, narrowing, creeps the sure encroaching doom.

ALL MOTHER

If I had an eagle's wings,
  How grand to sail the sky!
But I should drop to the earth
  If I heard my baby cry.
My baby—my darling,
  The wings may go, for me.

If I were a splendid queen,
  With a crown to keep in place,
Would it do for a little wet mouth
  To rub all over my face?
My baby—my darling,
  The crown may go, for me.

IN THE GARDEN

LINGERING late in garden talk,
  My friend and I, in the prime of June,
The long tree-shadows across the walk
  Hinted the waning afternoon.
The bird songs died in twitterings brief;
The clover was folding, leaf on leaf.

Sweetest season of all the year,
  And sweetest of years in all my time,
Earth is so bright, and heaven so near,
  Sure life itself must be just at prime.
Soft flower faces that crowd our way,
Have you no word for us to-day?

Each in its nature stands arrayed:
  Heliotropes that drink the sun;
Violet shadows that haunt the shade;
  Poppies, by every wind undone;
Lilies, just over-proud for grace;
Pansies, that laugh in every face.

In the Garden

Great bloused peonies half adoze;
 Mimulus, wild in change and freak;
Dainty flesh of the China rose,
 Tender and fine as a fairy's cheek.
(I watched him finger the folds apart
To get at the blush in its inmost heart.)

Lo, at our feet what small blue eyes!
 And still as we looked their numbers came
Like shy stars out of the evening skies
 When the east is gray and the west is flame.
" Gather, yourself, and give to me
These ' forget-me-nots,' " said he.

Word of command I take not ill;
 When love commands, love likes to obey;
But, while my words my thoughts fulfil,
 " Forget me not," I will not say.
Vows for the false; a loyal mind
Will not be bound, and will not bind.

In your need of me I put my trust,
 And your lack of need shall be my ban;
'Tis time to remember, when you must,
 Time to forget me when you can.

Yet cannot the wildest thought of mine
Fancy a life distuned from thine.

Small reserve is between us two;
   'Tis heart to heart, and brain to brain.
Bare as an arrow, straight and true
   Struck his thought to my thought again.
"Not distuned; one song of praise,
First and second, our lives shall raise."

Close we stood in the rosy glow,
   Watching the cloudland tower and town;
Watching the double Castor grow
   Out of the east as the sun rolled down.
"Yonder, how star drinks star," said he;
"Yield thou so—live thou in me."

Nay, we are close—we are not one,
   More than those stars that seem to shine
In the self-same place, yet each a sun,
   Each distinct in its sphere divine.
Like to Himself art thou, we know;
Like to Himself am I also.

What did He mean, when He sent us forth,
   Soul and soul, to this lower life,

Each with a purpose, each a worth,
   Each an arm for the human strife?
Armor of thine is not for me;
Neither is mine adjudged by thee.

See, in the lower life we stand,
   Weapons donned, and the strife begun;
Higher nor lower; hand to hand;
   Each helps each with the glad " Well done !"
Each girds each to nobler ends;
No less lovers because such friends.

So, in the peace of the closing day,
   Resting, as striving, side by side,
"What does He mean?" again we say;
   " For what new life are our souls allied?"
Comes to my ken, in death's advance,
Life in its next significance.

See yon tortoise, he crossed the path
   At noon, to hide where the grass is tall;
In a slow, dull sense of the sun-king's wrath,
   Burrowing close to the garden wall.
Think, could we flood that torpid brain
With man's whole life—love, joy, and pain !

In the Garden

So, methinks, is the life we lead
  To the larger life that yet shall be:
Narrow in thought, uncouth in deed,
  Crawling, who yet shall walk so free;
Walking, who yet on wings shall soar;
Flying, who shall need wings no more.

Lo, in the larger life we stand!
  We drop the weapon, we take the tool;
We serve with mind who served with hand,
  We live by law who lived by rule.
And our old earth-love, with its mortal bliss,
Was the fancy of babe for babe, to this.

Visions begone! About us rise
  The worlds, on their work majestic sent.
Down in the dew the small fire-flies
  Make up a tremulous firmament.
Stars in the grass, and roses dear,
Earth is full sweet, tho' heaven is near.

WHIPPOORWILL

(DELAWARE WATER GAP)

MAN

LIGHTS of gold—shades of brown;
Now the evening breeze is blurring
All our water-pictures, stirring
Seeming solid heath and hill.
Large and red, the sun rolls down;
Is he gone? Yet see, the same,
Air ablaze, waves aflame.
Hark! a voice upon the hill—
"Whippoorwill, Whippoorwill!"
I'm a scholar, by the way,
With a curious gift at learning,
By some natural, strange discerning,
Lore of wood and heath and hill.
I know all the creatures say;
I can render, as we walk,
The soliloquizing talk
Of yon pious Whippoorwill:
Hark! again—"Whippoorwill!"

46 ·

WHIPPOORWILL

BIRD

Whippoorwill, day is o'er;
Not a voice to break the quiet.
I must haste to profit by it,
—Softly, not to rouse the hill.
Breezes, hush! Waves, speak lower!
Twenty *ave's* I may win
Ere the rest their task begin.
"Whippoorwill, Whippoorwill."
(Silent, all!) "Whippoorwill."

Whippoorwill—that counts thirteen;
How remiss I find the others!
Were it not my duty, brothers,
To report you? Then I will.
Saints, indeed! What can it mean?
Hist—I hear low voices rise—
Would you take me by surprise?
Here I stand, thirteen gained;
"Whippoorwill, Whippoorwill!"

Dark and sweet. Star by star
From the river depth is rising;
Three more voices; 'tis surprising,
Such irreverence in the trill!

47

WHIPPOORWILL

" Whippoorwill," near and far.
Rattle, mumble, how they go.
I speak out, distinct and slow,—
" Whippoorwill, Whippoorwill,"
Listen, all : " Whippoorwill !"

Do they feel a word they say?
—Vesper voices fill the valley;
Now indeed 'tis time to rally;
Ha! they gain upon me still.
Use decorum, brothers, pray!
Not so loud—keep your place—
Feel more reverence—what a pace!
Take your time—hold your tongue—
" Whippoorwill, Whippoorwill !"

MUCH ADO ABOUT NOTHING

REQUEST

THE red day is melting into even,
  And the even looks on you and me alone,
As you stand tall and clear against the westward,
  With heaven's glory added to your own.

The sun creeps ablaze among your tresses,
  The winds press unchidden to your brow;
If you ever mean to give me what you promised,
  I am ready for it now:—give it now.

The sun greets the earth before his parting,
  The waves kiss the shore and trip away,
And cloud leans to cloud across the heaven,
  And I wonder you can dare to answer nay.

By the brown stars that bend in mocking o'er me,
  By the brown clouds that loosen on your brow,
By the wreathed lips that taunt me with their redness,
  I am sworn to have it now:—give it now.

MUCH ADO ABOUT NOTHING

REFUSAL

The last words I gave you when we parted,
  My last words for evermore shall be :—
You may borrow all the sweets of all the summer,
  But you'll never borrow kisses, sir, from me.

I lend not, I sell not, I give not;
  And yet they are to me as little worth
As the common drops or rain, before the sun-god
  Has spanned with them the heaven and the earth.

The young moon is weaving spells around us;
  The sweet darkness witches us to stay;
The late darkness creeping all around us
  Is warning us away:—come away.

You would surely never take what I deny you,
  And yet it were a sin to break a vow:
But if you *meant* to steal it, as I fear me,
  You had better do it now:—take it now.

RAIN-DAYS

THE warm Spring rains, bloom-pregnant, slip to
     earth,
Melting black Winter into rosy May.
The sudden Summer rains come hurrying down,
Eager with great quick drops to satisfy
The heat-split grass, and choking, gasping dust
That drinks and drinks, and lies at last content.
The wild Fall rains rush down like mailèd hosts;
Spoil the bird-homesteads, and tramp out the flowers,
And rot the forests.   Then chill Winter rains,
Sad Winter rains, dead Winter rains, each drop
A ghost of old Spring freshness.   All to-day
Winter wept cheerlessly, but I, within,
Sit far from cheerless, while the outside night
Contests my hearth-light, peopling all the room
With dancing flames and shadows.

               What am I
But ghost of old Spring freshness?   Yet not so;
That poor old wandering wind goes sobbing by,
Still doting on the unresponsive earth,
Still calling, scolding, pleading; not one flower

Rain-Days

Will the clay answer.   Is the earth then dead?
Is she then old? not so; from that vast heart
There rose no last Spring's bloom but left its seed
In the same bosom; not a forest chief
Dropped, shred by shred, his leafy glory down,
But she will make of them his future crown.
She never lost a leaf, but in herself
Garners all seasons as they seem to die.
So have I garnered in my deepening heart
My seasons as they came; so stand I now,
Dead to world-calls, and listening momently
For my Spring summons to an unknown land.
And these wild nights, when outside cold and dark,
Make home and hearth so dear, I sit and read
In the quick coals all far-off memories
Of home, wife, children; each new love that came
Building its cell of sweetness in my heart,
Which must be full as then until I die.
Friends, children, all are gone; I am so old:
But still, and much of late, they come again,
And still the dead rain falls, and in its sound
I hear the music of old rain-days gone.

God bless the rain-days! Just as dark a time
Gave a pet brother to my love and care.

That strange dull afternoon they called me up
To the death-chamber, when about my neck
My mother, she a widow, wound her arms
And drew my face to hers, and gave her child,
Her last and darling, to my boyish care.
Sure the kind Father must have smiled to see
The uncouth work, as I—a schoolboy lump
Of brawling crudeness—all at once put on
A parent's anxious looks and careful ways.
Ah, sweet to rest come memories of past strife,
And sweet to placid age youth's conquered cares,
Pains alchemized to joys, ease born of throes,
Old loves forever new.—My brother gone,
We had grown old together, yet wert thou
Still young to me, my friend, my mate, my care.
Still gentle, trustful, woman-natured. Now
God and thy mother keep thee; Watch for me.
Still drop the echoes of old rain-days gone.
I see a woodpath, and a broken shed
Raised by some woodman of an earlier time;
Its rude, low roof, age-thick with pulpy moss,
Its walls a mass of forest vines; above,
The skies are all in conflict; lumbering clouds,
Rallied too suddenly, come rolling up
In huge confusion, leaving here and there

Rain-Days

Odd patches of astonished blue; anon
They stoop and mingle, and the first drops fall
Crisp through the hot leaves. Not alone I sit
Storm-prisoned; there's a dear hand clasped in mine,
Clasped first that day. My fearful eager eyes
Fasten on eyes most earnest and serene,
Looked into first that rain-day, when the storm
Surprised us on our way: so many times
My struggling heart had yielded to its fears,
And left the love-words budding on my lips
Frost-caught ere one had blossomed into speech.
And yet not bashful she; a flippant word
Had power to flush her cheek; a passing glance
Could make her spirit shrink; but never called
A soul to hers in truth and gravity,
And went unanswered; so, as still my tongue
Fared faltering through its story, in her eyes
Sat a strong, quiet angel, aiding me.

Thus long we sat, half dreaming, half aware,
The while, unnoted then, remembered now,
From change to change, from plunging seas of rain
To quiet drippings; all at once a beam
Of full, triumphant sunset broke our dream.
Then, slowly taking thought, we planned to live

More highly for each other; planned to weave
Our courtship close with friendship; humbly vowed
To let no pride between us, no light word,
A thought, a film, a veil, an air-built wall
To shut us from each other unaware.
So, as we sat, the little shed became
A sanctuary, and all the air was rife
With unseen being, till the blessing closed
Round us, within us, blending soul with soul
For an eternity,—two loves, two lives
In one,—my lesser heart absorbing hers
As lies some bounded lake and holds all heaven.

My Mary! Back through ranks of outworn years,
Through dulling age to youth, I reach to seize
This memory; up through death and time to thee
I send it as a greeting; Watch for me.

A MERRY OLD SOUL

Loose foolish lips; wrinkled eyelids,
Hiding the rheumy eyes within;
White dirty hair upon his forehead,
White dirty stubble on his chin.
He lodges with a friend, in the cellar,
The cellar door his roof and his throne:
'Tis last night's merry old toper,
Musing this morning alone.

" Last night we had a roaring supper;
Last night I sang a jolly song;
Now 'tis the miserable morning,
And all's changed, and all seems so wrong.
I can't work, I'm not fit—too shaky;
I can't find my other shoe; I'll try;
—I won't try; it makes me unhappy.—
Suppose I should end it all, and die.

" The hearse takes you up—of course, no mourners;
And Jake airs the lodgings—no, he'd save
To dig me in at once, in the cellar;
Worms there, most likely, for a grave.

56

But then there's the water, that's improper,
And most like unwholesome;—by the way
There's quite too much water (and I'll say it
To his face) for the rent we have to pay.

" And just look at that now—my sunshine
Gone to the other cellar door!
Ugh, but I'm chilly!—it's always
Such a hard world for the poor.
There's a good bone by the gutter,
Still, it's a trouble; if I try
Will that strange dog let me eat it?
See how he watches—let it lie.

" Who made a beast of me, I wonder?
Jake, maybe, tampering with my gin?
No! tavern politics,—that brought me
Down to his clutches, to begin.
Wait . . . 'Twas the Colonel's little dinners;
Prime fellows—ladies all away.
Ha! 'twas my mother, at her table,
Toasting her little boy in play.

" Here comes a lady—and clean, too;
Like . . . Who was that I used to know?

A Merry Old Soul

—Well, maybe some of ours, mud lilies,
Picked young, would make as fair a show.
But this one's a lady.   How she stands there!
Ain't you ashamed to look at me?
—Damn you! take your eyes off,—they hurt me,—
And yet, why care?   Let it be."

ALICE

WHAT shall we do with Alice?
　　Our youngest and our pride,
And yet she brings us more of care
　　Than all the world beside.
She is the only drone of five,
　　A lovely, useless thing,
With a heart as rich as summer,
　　And a face as fresh as spring.

What *can* we do with Alice?
　　She idles so at school;
She decks with buds the good dame's cap,
　　And fears nor rod nor rule.
And while her sisters o'er their books
　　With puzzled, earnest faces pore,
She makes a baby-bower of leaves
　　Beside the school-house door.

She will not heed the morrow;
　　She will not take to care:
Her eyes, like suns, make every cloud
　　Their laughing colors wear.

ALICE

And if the earth be green or bare,
  And if the sky be dark or clear,
She carries with her everywhere
  Her own bright atmosphere.

My idle, aimless Alice!
  She'll waste the livelong day,
Where quivering gold and shadows
  O'er the lazy lilies play.
Where great trees guard the silver song
  That lapses ever tinkling by,
And round its bank the violets throng
  To see the mirrored sky.

She looks up to the stranger
  With her arms upon his knee;
She smiles upon the Master,
  Though a dreaded man is he:
She shrinks not from the crawling worm,
  Nor startles at the wood-snake's hiss:
She shouts to hear the rolling storm,
  In strange enraptured bliss.

That tree the wind uprooted,
  And flung across the stream,

ALICE

She found to-day, and left her play,
    Amid its boughs to dream.
With bare feet in the water,
    And arms bathed deep in flowers,
She carols, smiling to herself,
    Through all the happy hours.

My fearless, wilful Alice!
    We cannot make her shrink,
Nor hide her face with bashful grace,
    Nor fear what others think.
She is too sure of kindly looks
    To learn another's eye to shun:—
But GOD, who hid the violet, bade
    The rose stand in the sun.

My useless, aimless Alice!
    Yet from those night-blue eyes
Strange thoughts oft step forth lazily,
    Like stars from darkening skies:
And sudden tones have sanctified
    The little songs she sung;
And simple words, that seem inspired,
    Have faltered from her tongue.

ALICE

At early even, kneeling
   In the holy twilight gloom,
When songs are hushed and prayers go round,
   And blessings fill the room:
We plead for health and common joys,
   To all the rest:—for *her* we say,
" We know her not; whate'er her lot,
   Dear GOD, be Thou her stay."

AN OUTCAST

I saw a stately dwelling, all alight,
Beaming forth pleasure from its many eyes
Till night was fain to smile; and one without
Stood gazing on the joyful revellers,
Like a lost angel peering in at heaven.
A woman, yet not woman; on her face
Beauty sat mourner for lost loveliness.
A woman, but her bright mouth sin had kissed,
And branding out the sweetness, left the rose.

She leaned against the window, and gazed long
Upon the deepening revelry; her ear
Drank in the music of fresh happy voices,—
Music that turned to discord as it fell
Among her memories; then a bitter stream
Rose from the poisoned fountain of her soul,
And poured itself in words.

    " Sing on, laugh on,
Poor self-complacent clay—poor feeble cloud

Of insects glittering gay in fortune's sun!
How brave ye shine, unknowing ye are dust,
Secure in untried virtue; if but once
Temptation fell upon you like a storm,
How many proud would fall dismayed to earth,
How many pure would rise with soilèd wings,
Of those who, were I now to seek their feet,
Would shriek, and faint, and shun my touch like
    death?

"Ye fools! was ever yet a flower so pure
That did the wanton sun shine hot enough
He could not wither? Ye are only flowers;
The world's few stars, the few high burning
    hearts
O'er whom sin never found a talisman,
They are too brave to spurn or fear the fallen,
But dare to smile on all.—O God! kind God!
But would they smile on me? If I could kneel
To ask heart-charities, is there one hand
Would raise me? If I tear it from my heart,
This old sin-cancer, is there one would pour
Soft words instead of scorn upon my wounds?
Too well I know, not one. Then, heart, be calm,
And rock thy sins to rest; there's still a joy

For those who cannot rise,—it is to fall;
To cast off hope, as divers doff their garments,
And, plunging headlong, sound the depths of sin.

" Stand back, thou craven conscience, 'tis too late !
Away, thou traitor shame, I know thee not !
I'll hide my hunted soul in wickedness,
As some poor sun-tormented traveller
Leaps in the poisoned stream. And at the last,
When life and death are dead, and GOD is all,
Sitting to square accounts 'twixt earth and heaven,
When every soul shall plead its puny cause,
I will stand up and say, ' LORD, curse the world,
For they have *all* transgressed against thy law.
My heart was thirsting for a drop of kindness
On its steep, lonely journey back toward heaven,
And they refreshed me not; my soul was naked,
Shrinking and trembling in its shame, and calling
Most piteously for shelter from the eyes
Of tittering virtue, and they clothed me not.'

" Then GOD will smile to see the frightened looks
Of those who thought their places sure in heaven;
And Satan laugh to greet the trooping souls

An Outcast

Of those who had denied him on the earth.
Then . . . Ah! my traitor heart, my cruel heart,
How canst thou, with thy melting memories,
Steal from me this poor fancy of revenge?

" The years come rushing backward like a flood:
I see a dear, time-tinted cottage peep
From out a whispering luxury of leaves;
I see a little child upon the door-sill,
Where, in the sleepy afternoon, the sun
Strives lazily to pass the shadows, making
All hues of gold and green; she sits alone,
Her rosy little cheek upon her hand,
Spelling out ' S-i-n' in the old story book,
And wondering what it means:—Can this be I?

" The years roll back upon me like a flood.
I see a stately girl, with delicate brow,
And eager eyes that look upon the world
Expecting nought but truth:—Can this be I?
Sure I am young and pure again—old thoughts
From that sweet time when all my thoughts were
    hopes,
Fall like a shower of violets on my brain.

An Outcast

There is an angel busy at my heart,
Searching its corners and dark crevices
For virtues crushed and lost among its scars.

"Lost? No, they live! I hear the GOD-breathed
　　voice
That as I lay awake at dead of night
Said, 'Soul, thou art immortal; sin was made
For thee to vanquish; as a mother's love
Denies her clinging child, and sets afar
The tottering feet that so must learn their use,
From thee, my well-beloved, I recede,
That so by striving thou shalt reach to me,
And grow thereby.'

　　　"Ah, soul, did I not strive?
Did I not conquer? Thou, who knowest all,
Did ever Satan find more subtle means
To snare one child? Yet with what zeal of youth
Did I and Want, embracing, turn our backs
Upon the host of ugly, petted sins
That crawl to earth's high places — with what
　　schemes
Of glorious, living, daily martyrdom

AN OUTCAST

I fashioned out the future—all in vain,—
O yearning, striving years, and all in vain!

" Just GOD, where lagged thine angels, when at last,
  Amid my prayers, amid my victories,
  One slinking, masked crime, so masked, it seemed
  A virtue, with its sudden backward thrust
  Murdered my soul?"

ANOTHER CHANCE

I LEAN from my window above the river,
  To watch the winds and the waves at play;
But still as I watch, the waves forever
  Slip from my gaze and glide away.

Stay, blithe wind, and stand, fair river,
  And leave me never, thou dear To-day!
But still as I ask, the hours forever
  Slip from my life, and glide away.

I lose the waves, till my eyes are weary;
  They will not tarry, they seek the main.
On, still on! is their chorus cheery,
  Soon we shall blend and rise again.

I lose my days, till I stand despairing,
  For those were idle, and these are vain;
Yet hope, my heart, for the time is nearing,
  When I may live my life again.

EVENING THOUGHTS

O SUNLESS, cheerless day! The doleful clouds
Have wept and wept; the wind, with ceaseless whine,
Has wandered through the rain; now stooping low
To plague the sullen stream; now whirling high,
And diving down some chimney, where the dame
Strove vainly for a cheerful evening fire,
Beating the smoke into her patient face.
Now skimming earth so swift, that the long grass
Grows shrill with pain; now blustering past the
      flowers
And through the angry corn; now to the stream,
Making the willows sulk, and flounce, and trail
Their wet arms on the ground; now, scorning earth,
He's up to fight the clouds. Good wind, sweet wind,
Battle them sore—scatter the enemy
That we may gain the farewell of the sun,
And catch the blessing. Joy! The weary foes
Have raised the siege, and now, dispersing slow,
Retire; the trees, all dripping, stand ablaze,
Thrilled by the cordial light, that suddenly
Enclasping, sets each separate soft green leaf

Quivering with life; till, with majestic joy,
They fling on high their bold ambitious arms
In hope to touch the skies that seem so near.
The loving clouds bend downward from the blue,
And form, and melt, and break like hills of foam,
Paling to silver,—blushing back to rose;
Gathering in mountains of rich purple glooms;
Deepening to awful caverns and strange chasms;
Then breaking, softening, melting, till the sky
Grows dark, and deep, and clear, and a keen eye
Can almost reach to heaven, whence issuing forth,
With their fresh glory on them, oue by one,
The great stars take their places, and poor earth
Stands in the presence of the universe.
Shrink back, thou small mean orb, into the dark;
Heaven passes; veil thee close with leaves and clouds!

Yet I would rather live thy life, sweet earth,
With human woes and joys, than be a star
Hard smiling in cold beauty, bright and bleak.
I envy not your glory, proud, pale stars,
Each on a separate throne,—do ye not pine,
Flinging your dark arms vainly through the blank,
For some sweet human touch? Do ye not yearn,
Searching through space with sadly burning eyes,

Evening Thoughts

For our poor leaf-clad orb, where some small flower,
Leaning its cheek against another near,
Loves its frail life away? What's life but love?
What soul in highest heaven can more than love?

O earth, whose sighs are sweet, whose cares are dear,
Whose smiles, like rainbows, live more bright for
      tears,—
Most precious earth, I hail thee! This fair night,
While yet my keen-strung soul, like some rough
      harp
Thrilled with a breath from heaven, swells high and
      loud
With music not its own I sing to thee:—
Of woods and waters, glorious in the sun:
Of flowers and fountains, yielding their fair lives
In beauty and in light; of daily smiles
Poured from the founts of ever-flowing love,
On ever-thirsting hearts; of summer eves,
When heaven brings kindly close to harvest day
And bids the laborer rest; of children's voices
Ringing their welcomes from his waiting door;
Of sunsets Catholic, that pour at large
Cathedral glory into cottage panes.
Shadows and stars and music for earth's night;

Sunshine and flowers and laughter for her day;
And love for all. Thou Life, who sit'st above,
Creating life, aye, sprinkling space with worlds
From Thy dim fingers,—not so much for these
I bow to Thee, as that in this far earth
Thou hast made human hearts, and taught them
     love.
For Love, she is invincible; through her,
Frail, faltering man, brave, struggling, conquering
     man,
Towers o'er the angels innocent and untried;
And Love, she is omnipotent; no soul
Without her tending, could outlive its clay,
So brutish else, and weak. We wake, and sleep;
We hunger, and are cold; we grow, and die;
We strive with weaker brothers for their spoils,
And yield to stronger; spider-like we toil
And plot to snare our fellows; or, like ants,
We build wise plans, and stand in blind amaze
To find them crushed beneath Fate's iron heel;
We strive, and fail; we reason, and are lost;
We love,—and we touch God.

COMPENSATION

I AM not a prosperous man;
    The ships I send to sea
Are apt to meet some strange defeat
    Ere they come back to me.
And her eyes are dulled with care;
    And the castle that serves our prime
Is a poor affair to those in the air
    We built in our courting time.

This morning, waking slow
    To a sense of the coming day,
Of the life too mean, and the might have been,
    My coward heart gave way.
My heart appalled sank down;
    But rose again with a leap
At our delight when at dead of night
    Our babe laughed out in his sleep.

AN OLD MAID

Sitting in the twilight,
  Looking out into the rain,
Through the blurred and dripping dimness
  Of my window-pane:
Waiting in the chilly twilight
  For the supper bell to ring,
Float a flood of fancies o'er me—
  Thoughts of the Spring.

Oh, the early Spring-time!
  In the woodlands, even now,
Life is rising, tightly swelling
  Twig and bulb and bough.
Through the clods the moss is pushing;
  Homeward birds are on the wing;
Earth is quick with coming glory—
  Oh, for the Spring!

Spring has something sweeter;
  Leaves unfolded thick and brown,
Bursting soon, will drop their shadows,
  Trembling softly down.

An Old Maid

Buds will bloom and skies will deepen;
   Water flash and woodlands ring;
Through long grass the brooks will rustle—
   Oh, for the Spring!

Life has something sweeter;
   Strange, to feel old fancies start,
Violet-sweet, of youth and passion,
   From my wrinkled heart:
May agone, whose flowers were kisses—
   May, whose songs but one could sing;
Heart abloom, so sudden blighted—
   Ah, my lost Spring!

Still something sweeter;
   There's a home-love underlies
Passion, as the fruit that greatens
   When the blossom dies.
Plans of homestead, long forgotten!
   Plans that fancy used to bring
Round me in the fragrant twilight
   Of my lost Spring.

Still something sweeter;
   Other dreams about me stand;

An Old Maid

Thrills a round cheek on my bosom—
  Feels a little hand.
Baby eyes in mine are smiling;
  Baby fingers round me cling;
Baby lips are lisping " Mother"—
  God! my lost Spring.

MISMATED

A COMMON spring of water, sudden welling,
Unheralded, from some unseen impelling,
  Unrecognized, began his life alone.
A rare and haughty vine looked down above him,
Unclasped her climbing glory, stooped to love him,
  And wreathed herself about his curb of stone.

Ah, happy fount! Content in upward smiling,
To feel no life but in her fond beguiling,
  To see no world but through her veil of green!
And happy vine, secure in downward gazing,
To find one theme his heart forever praising—
  The crystal cup a throne, and she the queen!

I speak. I grew about him, ever dearer;
The water rose to meet me, ever nearer;
  The water passed one day his curb of stone.
Was it a weak escape from righteous boundings,
Or yet a righteous scorn of false surroundings?
  I only know I live my life alone.

Alone? The smiling fountain seems to chide me—
The constant fountain, rooted still beside me,
  And speaking wistful words I toil to hear;
Ah, how alone! The mystic words confound me;
And still the awakened fountain yearns beyond
      me,
  Streaming to some unknown I may not near.

"Oh, list," he cries, "the wondrous voices calling!
I hear a hundred streams in silver falling;
  I feel the far-off pulses of the sea—
Oh, come!" Then all my length beside him faring,
I strive and strain for growth, and soon, despair-
      ing,
  I pause and wonder where the wrong can be.

Were we not equal? Nay, I stooped, from climb-
      ing,
To his obscure, to list the golden chiming,
  So faint to all the world, so plain to me.
Now, 'twere some broad fair streamlet, onward tend-
      ing,
Should mate with him, and both, serenely blending,
  Move in a grand accordance to the sea.

MISMATED

I tend not so; I hear no voices calling;
I have no care for rivers silver-falling;
    I hate the far-off sea that wrought my pain.
O for some spell of change, my life new-aiming!
Or best, by spells his too much life reclaiming,
    Hold all within the fountain-curb again!

A HOUSEKEEPER'S TRAGEDY

ONE day as I wandered, I heard a complaining,
 And saw a poor woman, the picture of gloom;
She glared at the mud on her door-step ('twas rain-
  ing),
 And this was her wail as she wielded her broom:

"Oh! life is a toil, and love is a trouble,
 And beauty will fade, and riches will flee,
And pleasures they dwindle, and prices they double,
 And nothing is what I could wish it to be.

"There's too much of worriment goes to a bonnet;
 There's too much of ironing goes to a shirt;
There's nothing that pays for the time you waste
  on it;
 There's nothing that lasts but trouble and dirt.

"In March it is mud; it's slush in December;
 The midsummer breezes are loaded with dust;
In Fall the leaves litter; in muggy September
 The wall-paper rots and the candlesticks rust.

6   81

A Housekeeper's Tragedy

"There are worms in the cherries, and slugs in the
     roses,
    And ants in the sugar, and mice in the pies;
The rubbish of spiders no mortal supposes,
    And ravaging roaches, and damaging flies.

"It's sweeping at six, and it's dusting at seven;
    It's victuals at eight, and it's dishes at nine;
It's potting and panning from ten to eleven;
    We scarce break our fast ere we plan how to dine.

"With grease and with grime, from corner to centre,
    Forever at war, and forever alert,
No rest for a day, lest the enemy enter—
    I spend my whole life in a struggle with dirt.

"Last night, in my dream, I was stationed forever
    On a little isle in the midst of the sea;
My one chance of life, with a ceaseless endeavor,
    To sweep off the waves ere they swept over me.

"Alas! 'twas no dream—again I behold it!
    I yield; I am helpless my fate to avert."—
She rolled down her sleeves, her apron she folded;
    Then lay down and died, and was buried in dirt.

IF

Oh, were I a billow, a billow,
  And thou my shore should be,
I'd gather my measure of ocean treasure,
  And dance myself to thee;
    I'd leave the winds aside,
    And lead the lagging tide,
Resting never and dancing ever,
  To fling my life on thee.

Oh, were I a lily, a lily,
  And thou my charmèd bee,
I'd lure thee, and love thee, and close above thee,
  And ne'er would set thee free;
    The wrathful sun might pale,
    The scolding winds might rail,
So, dying together, my leaves should wither
  O'er thee, my love, o'er thee.

Oh, were I a willow, a willow,
  And thou my breeze should be,
Still closer creeping, each small leaf steeping,
  Till all were filled with thee;

If

Or rise in wrathful gale,
　And roar through all the vale,
I'd fling, imploring, my arms adoring,
　And bow, oh, storm, to thee.

Oh, were I a roselet, a roselet,
　And thou my sun should be,
I'd gather the sweetness of June's completeness
　In one red kiss for thee;
　　My heart would stand a-swoon
　　For pure excess of June,
Till, flushed with fulness, athirst for coolness,
　It burst at last to thee.

A LITTLE GOOSE

THE chill November day was done;
　The working world home faring:
The wind came roaring down the street
　And set the gas-lights flaring.
And helplessly, and aimlessly,
　The scared old leaves were flying;
When, mingled with the soughing wind,
　I heard a small voice crying.

And shivering on the corner stood
　A child of four or over:
No cloak nor hat her small soft arms
　And wind-blown curls to cover.
Her dimpled face was stained with tears;
　Her round blue eyes ran over;
She cherished in her wee cold hand
　A bunch of faded clover.

And, one hand round her treasure, while
　She slipped in mine the other,
Half-scared, half-confidential, said,
　" Oh, please, I want my mother."

A Little Goose

"Tell me your street and number, pet;
    Don't cry; I'll take you to it."
Sobbing she answered, "I forget;
    The organ made me do it.

"He came and played at Miller's step;
    The monkey took the money;
I followed down the street, because
    That monkey was so funny.
I've walked about a hundred hours
    From one street to another;
The monkey's gone, I've spoiled my flowers;
    —Oh, please, I want my mother."

"But what's your mother's name, and what
    The street?—now think a minute."
"My mother's name is Mother Dear;
    The street—I can't begin it."
"But what is strange about the house,
    Or new, not like the others?"
"I guess you mean my trundle-bed,
    Mine and my little brother's.

"Oh, dear, I ought to be at home
    To help him say his prayers;

A Little Goose

He's such a baby, he forgets;
  And we are both such players;
And there's a bar between, to keep
  From pitching on each other,
For Harry rolls when he's asleep;
  —Oh, dear, I want my mother!"

The sky grew stormy; people passed
  All muffled, homeward faring.
" You'll have to spend the night with me,"
  I said at last, despairing.
I tied a 'kerchief round her neck.
  —" What ribbon's this, my blossom?"
" Why, don't you know?" she smiling said,
  And drew it from her bosom.

A card, with number, street, and name!
  My eyes astonished met it;
" For," said the little one, " you see,
  I might some time forget it;
And so I wear a little thing
  That tells you all about it;
For mother says she's very sure
  I would get lost without it."

THE SEA AND THE STREAMS

Last night I crossed the sand, through mist and
    darkness,
To where, in some new spasm of expectation,
As if this time, at last, the land were yielding,
The sea heaved all his weight against the shore;
Then back he fled, with still the old amazement;
For still he could not pass the line God's finger
Had left along the sand: then fell to calling,
"More—more!" and league on league up-thundered,
    —" More!"

"O rivers, bring more life; O streams, assuage me;
Ye wells of freshness in the forests hiding,
And battling torrents white that rend the mountains,
And rock-pools gleaming on some Alpine crown,
Ye royal streams, on all your course attended
By forest nobles, with their choirs of music,
Ye underground blind lives, still groping seaward,
O fill my need; bring more—bring all—come down!"

All the dark world stood waiting for the morning;
But on heaven's face there seemed a hint of message

Which yet it must not speak.   No more in thunder,
But hollow-sweet, the sea.   " O waters, come!
Ye prisoned streams, break forth—in me is freedom;
Ye faltering, aimless streams, I am your mission;
Ye restless, seeking streams, I am your meaning;
Ye wandering, weary streams, I am your home."

Still in the starry dark the world stood waiting;
But in the conscious East, behold, the message;
A thrill, a flush, a miracle, a sunrise!
And ocean held his pulse.   Then came to me
Clear in that moment's glowing, awful silence,
From near and far a sound of answering voices,
A many-sounding song of waters moving
In universal cadence to the sea.

O wonderful! I heard the panting hurry
Of one fine rill that pushed beneath a pebble;
I heard the hollow plunge, down sunless gorges,
Of a lost cataract falling all alone;
I heard a meadow brook through long grass swashing;
I heard a garden fountain, tinkle, tinkle;
I heard the dreadful grating of the glaciers
In slow, vast movement down a world of stone.

THE SEA AND THE STREAMS

See, the far hills smile back the rosy message;
The tree-tops shine; from village chimneys rising,
Each dun smoke changes to a golden geyser;
The lark's wing flashes on his upward way.
Still calls the sea; the streams I hear no longer,
Lost in a rising swarm of sounds and voices;
For now a sea of light fills earth and heaven,
And all the joyful world awakes—'Tis day!

A CHILD'S EARLY LESSONS

SUMMER winds, Summer winds, where are ye hieing,
  Now that the bees and blossoms have flown?
The old leaves are dead, and the young leaves are
    dying,
  And I shall be left with the Autumn alone.
Stay, for I pine with this stately new-comer;
  Her breath is so chill, and her looks are so wan.
" Nay, little maid, we are friends of the Summer;
  Summer friends fly when the Autumn comes on."

Little birds, little birds, where are ye flying?
  Taking all music away in your tone:
The forests are fading, the flowers are dying,
  And I shall be left with the Autumn alone.
Stay, pretty songsters, and say for what reason
  You leave the poor child who has loved you so long.
" Nay, little maid, we are friends of the season;
  Summer friends fly when the Autumn comes on."

Roses, sweet crimson hearts, why are ye paling?
  Why in my path so rebukingly bow?

A Child's Early Lessons

Were ye not cherished with love never failing?
  Will ye not tarry and comfort me now?
We who have joyed in the sunshine together,
  Together will mourn now the glory is gone.
" Peace, foolish maiden, we change with the weather;
  Summer love cools when the Autumn comes on."

SEVENTEEN

WHILE the sweet Spring earth rejoices,
  And the forests, old and dim,
Populous with little voices,
  Raise their trilling hymn,—
Chime *our* songs in joyous pleading,
  With the music of the day,
We are young, and Time is speeding;
  Sweet Time, stay!

We would hold the hasty hours,
  Ope them to the living core,
Leaf by leaf, like folded flowers,
  Till they glow no more.
We are mated with the present;
  Bosom friends with dear to-day;
Loving best the latest minute;
  Sweet Time, stay.

Sovereign Youth! All dainty spirits
  Wait on us from earth and air;
From the common life distilling
  But its essence rare.

Golden sounds, to age so leaden;
  Eden sights, to age so drear;
Sweet illusions, subtle feelings
  Age would smile to hear.

Happy Youth! When fearless bosoms,
  With their wealth of follies rare,
Loose their thoughts, like summer blossoms,
  To the generous air.
When we sit and mock at sorrow,
  Looking in each others' eyes,
Greeting every new to-morrow
  With a new surprise.

Hope is with us, chanting ever
  Of some fair untried to-be;
Lurking Love hath prisoned never
  Hearts so blithe and free.
Yet, unseen, a fairy splendor
  O'er the prosing world he flings;
Everywhere we hear the rushing
  Of his rising wings.

As the tender crescent holdeth
  All the moon within its rim,

Seventeen

So the silver present foldeth
    All the future dim.
Ah, the prophet moon is sweetest,
    And the life is best to-day;
Life is best when time is fleetest;
    Sweet Time, stay!

THIRTY-FOUR

I CANNOT sing as once I sung
   When life with rhyme so close engaged,
When you and I were very young
   Instead of slightly middle-aged.

Then all my thought and all my song
   Were music, roses, honey-dew;
And most the dainty moonlight throng
   Of maiden fancies, strange and new.

All strange, yet true; as when we gaze
   In summer skies, their best to win,
What seemed the sky will part in haze,
   And show a deeper heaven within.

A deeper heaven—a deepening soul;
   Youth's rosy mist-wreaths pass away:
They bare new spaces as they roll,
   And depths unknown to yesterday.

And farther depths, and space more grand,
  And life increasing more and more,
As on each yesterday we stand,
  And grasp to-day, till youth is o'er.

Youth is not o'er; the ripe fruit holds
  The blossom's sweetness in its sphere:
The larger life the less enfolds,
  And nought is lost, but more is here.

And more will be; and more with time
  Life's scope and meaning we shall see,
And what shall keep the soul at prime
  Through all the far eternity.

A CAUTION

Love hailed a little maid
  Romping through the meadow;
Heedless in the sun she played,
  Scornful of the shadow.
" Come with me," whispered he;
  " Listen, sweet, to love and reason."
" By and by," she mocked reply,
  " Love's not in season."

Years went, years came,
  Light mixed with shadow;
Love met the maid again
  Dreaming through the meadow.
" Be not coy," urged the boy,
  " List in time to love and reason."
" By and by," she mused reply,
  " Love's still in season."

Years went, years came,
  Light turned to shadow;
Love saw the maid again,
  Waiting in the meadow.

A Caution

"Pass no more, my dream is o'er;
   I can listen now to reason."
"Keep thee coy," mocked the boy;
   "Love's out of season."

EXCEPTIONAL

Not by one gauge of fitness or unfitness
　　Judge we the lives around us, more than God
Asks of each plant the self-same bloom for witness
　　Of equal sunshine poured upon its sod.

And judge not him whose unfamiliar nature,
　　Higher or lower, differs from the rest;
Springs from the old seed in new form and stature;
　　Crosses the gardener's rules of worst and best.

Suppose one human form, embalmed for ages,
　　Were suddenly to catch its soul again;
To write anew, upon Time's later pages,
　　Its varied chronicle of joy and pain.

His heart brimful of memories and old yearning,
　　A quaint sweet harp, with none that know its tone;
His home-thoughts locked in long-forgotten learning,
　　And none can find the key; he is alone.

EXCEPTIONAL

He stands with outstretched arms, half sure, half
    fearing;
  He peers in every face with anxious eye;
He listens ever in the hope of hearing
  An echo to his call, but all pass by.

Yet welcome, though we comprehend not wholly
  His soul's strange idioms and peculiar needs:
Mayhap his hands, that learn our ways so slowly,
  Come bearing worthy fruits and precious seeds

From fields we know not: that far gaze, unheeding
  So oft the nearest gain, the moment's bloom,
Mayhap some word from GOD to man is reading,
  Which none would else interpret: give him room.

WAITING

Six: nay, at six, in any case
    He could not come; 'tis evening chime,
And if I reach the trysting place
    Whole hours before the trysting time,
'Tis not with any hope to see
    Unseemly soon my love appear;
He is no idle maid like me;
    He has high things to do and bear;
And not for worlds would I that he
For love should weakly eager be.

Seven: still an hour; not long to wait;
    But sixty minutes—fifty-nine,
Scarce time to quite anticipate
    My joy—not near enough, in fine.
And yet—it might be—some new chance,
    Some plot to take me by surprise—
If round yon rock a form should glance
    And strike on my astonished eyes!
Nay, down, my heart! It is not he;
True love must not impatient be.

Waiting

Eight: *now,* my heart! A step this way,
   . . . 'Tis past. Yon horse . . . It disappears.
A shout . . . 'Tis but the watch-dog's bay—
   Ah, he is playing with my fears,
Or sleep has held him over-long,
   (Could *I* sleep?) Or his friends detain,
(Would friends keep *me?*) Or duties throng;
   Or—see this sky—he hates the rain.
No, no; he keeps his tryst with me;
True love shall not suspicious be.

Nine: now by all I feel this hour,
   This is no love! and for my part,
I pray he never more have power
   To outrage thus a woman's heart.
Let him have never wife and child
   To waste their hours at window-pane;
Let him on no home-hearth be coiled
   To bask, and give no warmth again.
Gorge him with comforts—let him be
From love's least obligation free.

Ten: and the night grows black and chill;
   The way is long; the road is lone.
Who knows what thousand forms of ill
   May be along that pathway strewn?

WAITING

A stumbling horse; a secret foe;
   Even murder slinking on his track;
The strife in darkness—the last blow—
   Oh, would some chance might turn him back!
Peace; he is no poltroon like me:
His own right arm his guard shall be.

Eleven: 'tis o'er. My hope is gone!
   He will not come. My life is drear.
Aha, my love—my truth—my own,
   I knew—I knew you would be here!
Art hurt? Art weary? Rest thee now;
   Nay, rest and speak not, while I pour
Through living fingers on thy brow
   My too much life in thine once more.
Such thoughts I had—I blush to tell.
I see thy face and all is well.

FARM MUSIC

In the morning, dim and sweet,
  Slanting glints the sun;
The milkmaid trips with hurrying feet,
  The farmer's day is begun.
Hark! 'tis the mower blithe,
As he sharpens his trusty scythe,—
  Crink, crank—crink, crank!
In the dewy morning air.

In the summer, near to noon,
  Flaming climbs the sun;
The scythe-blades sweep to a pleasant tune,
  And the task goes merrily on.
Hark! shrill and fine,
The locust's hot-weather sign,—
  Cree-ee, cree-ee!
In the blazing morning air.

In the summer day at noon,
  Right over glares the sun;
The mowers sweep to a slower tune,
  And wish the task were done.

Farm Music

Hark! Hip—hurrah!
The dinner horn sounds afar,—
　Ta—tara—tara, tara!
In the seething noontide air.

In the lazy afternoon,
　Homeward looks the sun;
The meadow stream makes a tinkling tune,
　The mowers have nearly done.
Hark! a chattering loud,
'Tis the noisy crows in a crowd,
　Caw, caw, caw, caw!
Through all the hazy air.

The primrose wakes to bloom;
　Downward rolls the sun;
The west is fire, the east is gloom,
　The mowers' task is done.
And hist—hark!
What rings through the fragrant dark?
　Whippoorwill, whippoorwill!
Through all the evening air.

East and west are gloom,
　But the moon is rising fair;

And the night is warm, and the clover bloom
  Sweetens all the air.
And hist—hark!
Who calls through the silver dark?
  Hoo, hoo, tu whit, tu hoo!
Through all the midnight air.

AN ANGEL'S VISIT

She stood in the harvest-field at noon,
    And sang aloud for the joy of living.
She said: " 'Tis the sun that I drink like wine,
    To my heart this gladness giving."

Rank upon rank the wheat fell slain;
    The reapers ceased. " 'Tis sure the splendor
Of sloping sunset light that thrills
    My breast with a bliss so tender."

Up and up the blazing hills
    Climbed the night from the misty meadows.
" Can they be stars, or living eyes
    That bend on me from the shadows?"

" Greeting!" " And may you speak, indeed?"
    All in the dark her sense grew clearer;
She knew that she had, for company,
    All day an angel near her.

" May you tell of the life divine,
    To us unknown, to angels given?"
" Count me your earthly joys, and I
    May teach you those of heaven."

" They say the pleasures of earth are vain;
　　Delusions all, to lure from duty;
But while GOD hangs his bow in the rain,
　　Can I help my joy in beauty?

" And while he quickens the air with song,
　　My breaths with scent, my fruits with flavor,
Will he, dear angel, count as sin
　　My life in sound and savor?

" See, at our feet a glow-worm shines;
　　Lo! in the East a star arises;
And Thought may climb from worm to world
　　Forever through fresh surprises:

" And thought is joy.· . . . And, hark! in the vale
　　Music, and merry steps pursuing;
They leap in the dance—a soul in my blood
　　Cries out,—Awake, be doing!

" Action is joy; or power at play,
　　Or power at work in world emprises:
Action is life; part from the deed,
　　More from the doing rises."

"And are these all?" She flushed in the dark.
　"These are not all. I have a lover;
At sound of his voice, at touch of his hand,
　The cup of my life runs over.

"Once, unknowing, we looked and neared,
　And doubted, and neared, and rested never,
Till life seized life, as flame meets flame,
　To escape no more forever.

"Lover and husband; then was love
　The wine of my life, all life enhancing:
Now 'tis my bread, too needful and sweet
　To be kept for feast-day chancing.

"I have a child." She seemed to change;
　The deep content of some brooding creature
Looked from her eyes. "O, sweet and strange!
　Angel, be thou my teacher:

"When He made us one in a babe,
　Was it for joy or sorest proving?
For now I fear no heaven could win
　Our hearts from earthly loving.

"I have a friend. Howso I err,
  I see her uplifting love bend o'er me;
Howso I climb to my best, I know
  Her foot will be there before me.

"Howso parted, we must be nigh,
  Held by old years of every weather;
The best new love would be less than ours
  Who have lived our lives together.

"Now, lest forever I fail to see
  Right skies, through clouds so bright and tender,
Show me true joy." The angel's smile
  Lit all the night with splendor.

"Save that to Love and Learn and Do
  In wondrous measure to us is given;
Save that we see the face of God,
  You have named the joys of heaven."

THORNS

ONE rose, of all in the garden,
  I love the best to see.
To others, other are fairer,
  But this is queen to me.

Its thorns are many and sharp,
  But its blooms are many and fair;
And who would forego a rose,
  The pang of a thorn to spare?

Its thorns are many and sharp,
  But I well can bear the pain,
For they strike, and then, repenting,
  Are straight withdrawn again.

But once, and at unaware,
  A prickle, in sudden ire,
Burrowed into my hand,
  Keen as a point of fire.

And still it burns and rankles;
  I cannot still its ado:
Even to clasp a rose
  Quickens the sting anew.

THORNS

Even the tenderest touch
  Must give me only pain;
For this time, when it struck,
  It let the thorn remain.

I know, in a few to-morrows
  The hurt full healed will be:
'Twill be longer ere the rose
  Is quite the same to me.

AN OLD ROSE

As I wandered, lightly musing,
  Through the Roses in their pride,
Culling this, or that refusing,
  Casting many a bloom aside,
In my way a wilted flower
  Simpered still, and kept her ground;
Loth to lose her olden power,
  Loth to leave the belles around.

Fair, though wrinkled; sweet, though faded;
  Not a leaf had left its core:
Must she, then, by all unheeded,
  Through all time be known no more?
Is there any life for beauty
  After beauty's dreary close?
Death is sure the only duty
  Of a poor old Rose.

Still the Rose, her doom refusing,
  Smiling hides her blight and pain;
While each little wind at choosing
  Bares the unseemly spots again.

An Old Rose

Yield the spicy leaves, dear beauty,
  Ere their life to poison grows;
Spreading sweets is still the duty
  Of a poor old Rose.

Die, old Rose; and live forever
  Soul of scent that cannot die;
Live in every lover's favor,
  Every poet's minstrelsy.
Scatter thou, and I will gather,
  Standing fast, through winter's snows,
In a dream of summer weather
  From a poor old Rose.

AN OLD BUTTERFLY

His gorgeous plumes were a little worn;
One splendid wing was a trifle torn;
And the season waned. "How can it be
That I stand with my life unlived?" said he.
"Heigho!" said the butterfly,
"Would that I knew the reason why."

"Surely I loved the Violet pure,
And day by day to her nook obscure
I lowered my glorious wings, and quaffed
With a constant mind her perfumed draught.
But how strangely coarse her foliage grows;
Besides—at that moment I saw the Rose.

"I saw the Rose, and I knew my fate.
Slow she unfolded; I would not wait,
But prayed and fretted from hour to hour,
Till opened at last the perfect flower.
. . . A perfect flower? That cannot be,
Or how could she lose her hold on me?

An Old Butterfly

"For your Rose is burning sweet; in fine
  She is over-sweet to a taste like mine;
  Too rich, too much, to one who has seen
  In a garden beyond the Lily queen.
  I saw the Lily, and all was o'er:
  The Rose could reign in my heart no more.

"Creamy white is the perfect hue.
  Cold she seemed; with a great ado
  I won my welcome. Too late I see
  She cannot command the depths in me.
  Heigho!" said the butterfly,
  "What is it ails each love I try?"

And the season waned. No more he flies;
  On a Sunflower's bosom broad he lies.
  And after all, it is sad, we say,
  To think he has thrown himself away;
  Could it have been,—the reason why,
  That anything ailed the butterfly?

A LITTLE PROPHET

Spoke the nightingale to the rose,
   Once, so early in the morning,
Not a creature in all the glen,
Wearied and dull with a night of rain,
   Had perceived a warning.
" Yet," he said, " 'tis morning."

Night of rain, night of gloom;
   Ah, how sad for the birds a-building!
Soaking nests and blossoms torn,
And in all the east no sign of morn
   The weeping woodlands gilding.
" Yet," he sang, " 'tis morning."

" Nay, he raves," said the draggled flowers;
   " Sure, he raves," said the birds together.
Back to their streaming boughs they went,
Ragged and bunched with discontent
   At such unheard-of weather.
" Still," he sang, " 'tis morning."

"Waken," he cried, "ye creatures all,
   Violets, lift your dripping faces;
Bob-o-link, robin, arise and sing;
Choral larks, announce your king;
   Thrushes, choose your places;
For I am sure 'tis morning."

Darkness all; along the east,
   Hill on hill lay the awful thunder
—All in a flash, O wondrous sight!
Those dreadful gates of storm and night
   Burst and rolled asunder.
Lo, the Sun! 'Twas morning.

Back and back from their king they rolled;
   Grand he arose, and smiled around him.
Each small creature in wood and glen,
Blackbird, throstle, and tiny wren,
   Broke the spell that bound him.
"Joy!" they rang; "'tis morning."

Music and perfume everywhere;
   All the air in a golden glory;
Crowds of praisers fill the vale.
But really 'twas the nightingale
   Who first told the story.
He first said, "'Tis morning."

TO A FEW

PLAY-TIME for the young;
  Rest-time for the faint and old;
Soft leaves for the trees, now hung
  In rattling ice so cold;
Freedom for the sorely bound;
  Homes for those who would not rove;
For myself, the sweet world round,
  Give the boon of love.

Love is life—is GOD:
  Heaven is love, and lies around,
And the pathway oftenest trod
  Is its holiest ground.
So my hopes shall be as prayers,
  Not to some dim realm above,
But the heaven the lowest shares,
  To near hearts for love.

Love me for my love:
  Love is neither bought nor sold;
But itself its price can prove,
  Or itself can hold.

To a Few

I would ask it, as the sun
  Asks the earth through April hours;
Ye should give, as earth, full won,
  Makes reply in flowers.

Love me for my faults;
  Love me most, oh, brave and strong,
When my fainting spirit halts
  Weakly in the wrong.
Frailest tree needs firmest stay;
  Weakest child has closest care;
Dearest loved of Jesus, they
  Whose reproach he bare.

Love me when I doubt;
  When the heart's own self-mistrust
Compasses the soul about
  With a dimming rust.
" They will answer," Hope speaks clear;
  From the heart quick, sweet words come:
" Will they answer?" whispers Fear,
  And the lips are dumb.

" Shall they in surprise
  Put thy awkward proffer by,

To a Few

Or with careless words suffice
   Thy more earnest cry?"
So my doubts my heart would steel,
   Icing o'er its real glow:
Love me, friends, for what I feel,
   Not for what I show.

A PRISON HOME

O WEARY prison fortress
  Where year by year I lie,
Until the holy men have time
  To bring me out to die.
For still with blood and rack and fire
  The work upon their hands has grown;
And still I pine in dungeon cell
  Forgotten and alone.

Alone? What dimpled elbows
  Are leaning on my knee?
What sound of saucy laughter
  Fills all the air with glee?
My prison-born; she came to free
  Her mother's soul, and break her thrall;
So life by life my home has gone
  Till she and I are all.

Our prison sounds are loathsome
  To one who hears them long;
The murderer talking to himself,
  The drunkard's crazy song;

A Prison Home

But on my ear a prattle sweet,
  Or childish song forever rings;
Save when, in friendship's confidence,
  We talk of deeper things.

The jail-dogs are her playmates;
  The jailer is her thrall;
She finds a friend in every cell,
  And wins their best from all.
Within her sphere of innocence
  No evil thought will come,
And every face is kindly,
  And all the place is home.

Without, the world is changing;
  Some say, we make for liberty:
Meantime, the changes in her eyes
  Are all of life to me.
She's more to me than daily bread,
  And more than freedom after thrall.
My hope, my care, my comforter,
  My pet, my friend, my all!

THE SEASONS

ALL through the valley sweet music was sounding,
  Ringing the praise of the beautiful day.
Light through the valley a young child was bounding;
  'Twas dear little Spring, with the blossoms at play.
Schoolmaster Winter looked back at the singing:
  —" Child, I will teach thee a lesson to-day."
But Spring at the proser a violet flinging,
  Gloomy old Winter strode frowning away.

Oh, welcome to all was the little new-comer,
  And happy each wight in her favor to share:
So lovely she grew that they christened her Summer
  And thought she had wandered from paradise there.
" 'Tis shameful," growled Winter, " that she should
      be spending
  In mirth and in music the minutes so rare,
But weightier matters prevent my attending,
  So trusty aunt Autumn my message shall bear."

Cheerless and chill as the mission that bound her,
  Dreary aunt Autumn came forth to the day,

And wrapping a misty old mantle around her,
　　Harshly arrested the maid in her play.
" How can you sing while the season grows dimmer?
　　List to the lesson I'll read you to-day."
But as Autumn collected dead leaves for a primer,
　　Sweet merry Summer slipped laughing away.

DELAY

THE year's worst is done;
  The wild winter's over:
Through the barren March wind
  I smell the June clover.
Through the scolding March wind
  I hear the rose sighing,
And callow birds calling
  And old birds replying.

In the roaring March wind
  The rivers rise crashing,
The huge broken winter
  Down their fronts dashing.
And their moving is like
  To the freeing of a nation,
Rending a rule
  'Mid a world's jubilation.

Hist! through the ground
  There is stirring and groping,
Roots tingle, seeds thrill
  In the dark hoping.

127

DELAY

" Life, give us life!
   Through the grave's long dejection,
Sun, we believed!
   Sound now our resurrection."

Up the bare branches
   The life-blood is yearning.
In their cold forest nooks
   The creatures are turning.
" Is it time?" " Not yet;
   The frost lags belating."
—Oh, come, come, Spring!
   The world stands waiting.

INCONSTANT

I

In the forest darkness I heard a little fountain,
　　Gurgling alone at the closing of the day;
Came a thirsty shepherd-girl, weary from the moun-
　　　　tain,
　　Bent above the mossy curb and pushed the ferns
　　　　away.
Leaned across and drank, her hands together filling;
　　—Low laughed the fount, though the winds made
　　　　moan:—
Starts and looks again, stung with sudden thrilling,
　　Looking at her own name carven on the stone.

II

Winter came, winter passed: up spoke the fountain,
　　Telling strange tales of the darkness and the rain.
June brought the shepherd-girl, dancing from the
　　　　mountain,
　　Peering in the ferns for the happy word again.

INCONSTANT

When she stooped above the curb all the woods were
     ringing,
  —Low laughed the fount, while the winds made
     moan.—
When she rose, the air was dead; sudden ceased her
     singing—
Looking at the new name carven on the stone.

PRAYERS

A MOTHER prayed at the eventide
  With her child upon her breast.
The angels came to her darkened room;
  And waited her behest.

"And GOD," she asked, "Thou Glorious,
  O give my darling fame,
Among the nobles of his land
  To win the noblest name.

"And may there be some spirit near,
  My fervent wish to bear."
But the doubtful angels silent stood,
  Nor moved to waft her prayer.

"And GOD," she prayed, "Thou Infinite,
  O give my darling power;
The might of soul that sways a host
  As the fierce wind sways a shower.

131

"And may there be some spirit near,
    My soul's high wish to bear."
  But the wondering angels silent stood,
    Nor moved to waft her prayer.

"And God, who art all Beautiful,
    O make my darling fair,
  That he may still from life draw love,
    Life's sweetest essence rare.

"So every heart shall be a harp,
    Beneath his touch to sound."
  But the shuddering angels silent stood,
    And drooped their wings around.

"But if," she prayed, "Thou Merciful,
    He may not grasp at fame,
  O grant him strength to face serene
    A cold world's cruel blame;

"And if he shrink from earthly power,
    Nor aim to sway the time,
  Gird Thou his soul to cope with sin,
    A conqueror sublime.

" And if he sometime fail to strike
    Each heart to Love's sweet tone,
O may he tune to serap height
    The music of his own.

" Now may there be some spirit near
    My humble wish to bear."
The angels rose on rushing wings
    In haste to waft her prayer.

MY ROSE

WHEN the sun looks on it
    He makes it fair indeed ;
When the sun looks through it
    It doth all sun exceed.

When thou wert beloved
    I crowned thee with my love ;
Now thou also lovest
    Thou art all crowns above.

MY BROTHERS

I HAVE a sturdy brother that's very dear to me,
A little merry whirlwind that keeps the house in glee;
That keeps the house in torment, in wonder, and in
    dread,
For still the restless foot brings woe upon the golden
    head.

What makes the child so winning?   No wondrous
    gifts are here;
'Twill ever be a careless heart that lights those eyes
    so clear;
And yet that nameless charm I see that shall, as from
    a throne,
Sway higher souls and deeper hearts than e'er shall
    be his own.

I have a quiet brother, with deep'ning twilight eyes,
Where, as you gaze, new thoughts look forth, like stars
    from darkening skies;
With a rich low voice, and earnest look, that seems
    with gentle ruth
To plead with all for sympathy, and claim from all
    their truth.

My Brothers

My true, deep-hearted brother—yet if an impulse
    start,
A constant fear of cold repulse still checks the leap-
    ing heart;
And while, with yearning wild and strong, he fain
    would bare his soul,
A doubting, sullen bashfulness aye holds him in con-
    trol.

My shrinking, timid brother—yet far in those deep
    eyes,
A wealth of love, a might of scorn, a hate of mean-
    ness lies;
And when right bows, or great souls quail, or plotting
    small have sway,
The indignant angel scarce can bide its cramping
    bonds of clay.

My silent, haughty brother! I see thy trembling soul,
Like some fine strung Æolian, at every breath's con-
    trol,
Shrink proudly from the world's rude touch, and
    singing all alone,
They soon will sneer, because they hear no music in
    thy tone.

My Brothers

Alas for thee, my brother! I see the years press on,
A cold, dull crowd, with petty whips to beat thy spirit
    down;
Neglects shall crush, and falsehood goad with stings
    most keen and fine;
What duller hearts would bear unfelt shall eat like
    fire in thine.

Still it shall be thy fate to seek, and find no kin to
    thee;
To set thy mark too high, and mourn that others
    cannot see;
A stranger at thy mother's board—a pilgrim in thy
    land,
Whom many scorn, and some may love, but none will
    understand.

To strive, and fail; to love, and doubt; to trust, and
    suffer wrong;
To side with right, and fight for truth, and find but
    meanness strong;
Till thy sick tortured soul shall deem this sweet earth
    wholly vile—
God shelter thee, my brother! I will pray for thee
    the while.

AN APPEAL

FROM CELIE, MELIE, AND VELIE

By their next friend, ELIZA SPROAT TURNER

By permission of Lee and Shepard

WE are three tender, clinging things,
   With palpitating natures;
We can't endure that gentlemen
   Should think of us as creatures

Who dress like frights, and want their rights,
   Or business to attend to;
Or have their views, or ask the news,
   Or *anything* that men do.

O listen, valued gentlemen,
   Don't let yourselves be blinded;
We're not estranged, we're no way changed,
   And not the least strong-minded.

We can't abide careers and things;
   We never touch an 'ism;
We couldn't stand outside a sphere,
   Nor do a syllogism.

AN APPEAL

We don't enjoy rude health, like some,
 Nor mannish independence;
We're helpless as three soft-shelled crabs,
 Without some male attendance.

We need—oh, how we need!—a guide;
 Secure, his views obtaining,
Of what to like, and where to step,
 And whether it is raining.

And when we roam, we wait for him
 To point, with manly strictures,
The landscape out, and say, " Behold!"
 Just as they do in pictures.

We're trusting—confiding—
 Too easily we're blinded;
We're clinging, and hanging,
 And truly feeble-minded.

We disapprove the sort of girl
 Who calls for education,
And sells her talents, like a man,
 For bold remuneration.

An Appeal

We'd die before we'd learn a trade;
   We'd scorn to go to college;
We know (from parsing Milton) how
   Unfeminine is knowledge.

"God is thy law, thou mine," it says;
   Thou art my guide and mentor,
My author and my publisher,
   Source, patentee, inventor.

But we, we can do naught but cling,
   As on the oak the vine did;
And we know nothing but to love;
   Indeed, we're feeble-minded!

THE COMING WOMAN

By permission of Lee and Shepard

" WHAT will the coming woman do
    To plague, perplex, and interfere with us?
Will she forbid the festive chew
    And cuspidore for ages dear with us?
Will she invade, with lifted nose,
    Retreats where female foot ne'er went till late,
Bar-room cosey and court-room close,
    And force reluctant man to ventilate?"
        Brother, and so I hear.

" Will the dear haunts were manhood played
    At euchre bold, and frisky seven-up—
Haunts where so oft our reason strayed—
    To conversation teas be given up?
Must we, then, all go home to dine?
    And must a friend in soda pledge his mate?
How shall the coming man get wine
    At all, if she's allowed to legislate?"
        Brother, the case looks queer.

141

The Coming Woman

"Speak, O friend! has the woman's sphere,
    The soft-soap rainbow sphere we kept her in,
Burst and vanished, and left her here
    With the world at large to wield her sceptre in?
Is she up to our little game?
    And can she bind us, in reality,
Down to the precepts, much too tame,
    We've preached to her for pure morality?"
        Brother, the worst I fear.

"Friend of my youth, I can no more;
    Oh, fly with me this land iniquitous!"
Nay, for I see, from shore to shore,
    The enfranchised female rise ubiquitous.
Partner in purse she'll claim to be;
    Logic of business she'll outwit us in;
Lost from life is the dead latch-key,
    And lost from earth the white male citizen!
        Brother, the end is near.

A GIRL OF THE PERIOD

By permission of Lee and Shepard

I MET yesterday—I would you had seen her,
That wood-robin voice, that May-queen demeanor!
A wonderful girl; in her looks my ideal;
And yet from her curls to her boots she was real.

I know a queen rose from a daffy-down-dilly;
I know the good points of an unbroken filly;
I saw what she'd make, if once I had tamed her
To " smile when I praised" her, and. " weep when I
      blamed" her.

I said, " Lovely maid, do you know that your mission
On earth is to soothe man's uneasy condition?
To pour on the waves of his spirit's commotion
Your patience, forbearance, and general devotion?

" For man is so wild, so restless and raging,
His case seems to call for incessant assuaging;
And so a kind Providence makes your vocation
Consist out and out in amelioration.

"Moreover, the man is by nature despotic;
Resistance excites him to passions chaotic.
As you are all saints, while we are but human,
Obedience, etc., devolve on the woman.

"How sweet, when our passions enrage or betray us,
To keep one pure creature on hand to allay us!
Found out by a world which objects to receiving us,
To know there is one still obliged to believe in us!

"O maiden!" I cried, "don't you feel it your duty
To yield yourself up, in the May of your beauty,
Fulfilling your mission, dear feminine creature,
By merging yourself in my masculine nature?"

I looked in her face; not a blush was suffusing
The cheek that seemed dimpled by something
        amusing.
Then flashed her blue eyes, and if you'll believe it,
The shock was so great I could scarcely receive it.

"Young man," she replied, "I deplore most sincerely
The state of ill health you exhibit so clearly;
I would you were healed; but here my revolt is—
You may be a blister, but I'm not a poultice.

A Girl of the Period

" My life is so large, and its duties so various; -
I haven't the time to assume the vicarious.
Besides, you will find, when you reach Peter's wicket,
You can't enter heaven upon your wife's ticket.

" The man I shall wed, although faulty (he's human),
Is pure, or he's no mate for any pure woman;
And kind, or no love-needing heart would affect him;
And lord of himself, or no wife would respect him.

" In fine, we've concluded (this world to remodel)
No longer your foibles and vices to coddle;
For men will perforce, when they find all the sisters
Decline to be poultices, cease to be blisters."

She smiled as she passed, her answer completed.
—Now what way was that for a man to be treated?
It all comes of loosing the first of their fetters;
You yield the whole ground when you teach them
their letters!

WHAT TO DO.

"WHAT can a helpless female do?"
Rock the cradle, and bake and brew.

Or, if no cradle your fate afford,
Rock your brother's wife's for your board;

Or live in one room with an invalid cousin,
Or sew shop shirts for a dollar a dozen,

Or please some man by looking sweet,
Or please him by giving him things to eat,

Or please him by asking much advice,
And thinking whatever he does is nice.

Visit the poor (under his supervision);
Doctor the sick who can't pay a physician;

Save men's time by doing their praying,
And other odd jobs there's no present pay in.

146

But if you presume to usurp employments
Reserved by them for their special enjoyments,

Or if you succeed when they knew you wouldn't,
Or earn money fast when they said you couldn't,

Or learn to do things they'd proved were above you,
You'll hurt their feelings, and then they won't love
   you.